animals the size of dreams

animals the size of dreams

poems by

Lisa C. Krueger

RED HEN PRESS | Los Angeles, California

animals the size of dreams
Copyright © 2009 by Lisa C. Krueger

ISBN: 978-1-59709-145-1 (tradepaper)
ISBN: 978-1-59709-159-6 (clothbound)
Library of Congress Catalog Card Number: 2009904307

The Annenberg Foundation, the City of Los Angeles Department of
Cultural Affairs, the Los Angeles County Arts Commission, and the
National Endowement for the Arts partially support Red Hen Press.

Published by Red Hen Press
www.redhen.org
First Edition

Printed in Canada

Acknowledgements

Many thanks to *The Comstock Review, Lilliput Review, Pearl,* and *Rattle* for publication or acknowledgment of my poems.

Great appreciation and affection to my dear friends and family who offered literary and personal support: Kate, Mark, Ron, Maureen, Gretel, Priscilla, Paula, Cass, Chase.

Gratitude to my mentors in healing: Carla, Melissa, Bradford, Denise, Pam, Sally, Joy.

Love always to my family, Bob, Peter, Alex, Sally.

For Sally

Contents

I

II

III

IV

V

VI

And all amid them stood the Tree of Life,
High eminent, blooming ambrosial fruit
Of vegetable gold; and next to life,
Our death, the Tree of Knowledge, grew fast by –
Knowledge of good, bought dear by knowing ill.
                              —JOHN MILTON

. . . living in the orchard and being

hungry, and plucking
the fruit.
                              —DENISE LEVERTOV

animals the size of dreams

I

Harbor

(to seeds)

i scraped in silt
surrounding our lemon tree,

placed each of you
in a soft harbor,

covered you
with velvet brown blankets,

coffee can water,
my shadow

i didn't know
roots need space

to spread,
find their potential

still you came, emerged
from the small place of my faith,

and for a short time
bloomed

HAWK BLOSSOMS

to Kabir

Hawk. Twice you come to me,
seek me out in my kitchen
where I hide among steamy pots
of soup made from flowers and dirt

Blossoms push up through floor.
The ceiling cracks its fragile shell open to you.
I am afraid to die,
yet I unlock the door, let you in

Your pink breast against me,
your eye that has seen all
from so far above
bores deeply into mine

L.A. RURAL

Golden ooze is weakening our beams.
Buzz overpowers traffic, stirs up memories
of early urban farming,

how we watched crops grow from a Victorian porch
over drinks, everyone's kids playing tag half-naked
among dedicated stalks of corn.

Is that why we ignored this hum for years,
even when it grew louder,
drowned out everything?

A scented stain
descends the walls,
each room soft to touch.

STARFISH

after the diagnosis
my daughter's hands
are starfish,
long fingers
that taper
from
small
palms

when they touch
i gasp

i dream of being
a magician,
conjuring death
as a coin,
a bunny,
a scarf
disappearing
forever

JAVELIN HISS

Her doctor confides the illness can kill.
I return to afternoon under Cristo's umbrellas
where a woman near us died.
We drove against wind for hours
to witness hills of shimmering shelters,
art we could not miss.
At Tejon Pass we pulled over, climbed among them,
rested under one whose golden arc became
a world. We couldn't see beyond ourselves.
I ached from being full term with her,
from the way she rolled and tumbled with wind.
For pain I slipped into landscape.
When currents claimed one umbrella, I heard
the javelin hiss, a woman cry out,
did not notice it was me.

anything

but my girl—
the secret bargain out—

words silly bobbles at sea
in trivial formations.

i could not go on

clouds' sky skitter
responds *you will*

PERSEPHONE DELAYED

i am naked in the dark
of my daughter's room she sleeps
through the equinox i hear her breathe
rhythm of the world rivers
new lightwaves there is no
true light
in this room sun against curtains
by her bed i notice sketches she made
of prom dresses she won't wear photos
of hot guys from mags
scattered like petals on the floor
layers and layers where
she should walk she sleeps under
many robes only i am bare
she is breathing i tell myself
to breathe say to myself
you are breathing
say you must take this in
next let it out
i have lost all covering
raw in the darkness
breathing she breathes
i breathe
the unbearable blooms

Terror

not from stained sheets
or dry kisses
soft on the head.

not leg snakes
or tiger sweat,
echoes of jungle dark.

not rim of the seat
as it bangs the tank,
the break of storm trees

in the night.
not toilet bowl dance
with pink swirls.

the tremble
of hand
with sponge.

HOLLOW SOUNDS

My daughter in bed all day.
Outside, leaves fall out of season,
brittle notes of letting go.
She wears her ipod, I hear
the hollow sounds
of song as I pass by.
I can't stand music anymore,
the tune of anyone's voice.
I'd rather live in silence.
Ask this house to hold me,
its beams be my bones.
Ask for quiet.
Distant leaf blowers drone
making the world bare.

INSOMNIA

Sketch dreams to make time pass.
—journal entry

Page one, woman in my closet
counts daughter's pills.
Meds have feet,
one sleeps in her mouth.

Page two renders mother's ice garden.
She wears boxers, apron in snow,
sprays crystals on lilacs in bloom,
yet her tears won't freeze.

Page three: stick figure,
girl trying to fly, naked body
bloats, stretch marks
wide as wings.

Page four's crone with no navel
smiles Eden lips,
goes it alone with plants,
piston, stamen and all.

Can't stop looking,
songs I play for weeks.
Final page I dig in dark until drowsy
from moving moist grit.

Unearth baby, wrap her in leaves.
Can't get past her good intent
about to unfurl. Maybe this time
she will bloom.

RUBY

my earth, my air—
i excavate

with no guiding light
no hammer, chisel

my tool is bare bone.
i dig in weather not

summer or spring,
all around me

wither plants.
can't remember

the sear of birth,
how we laughed after

only this, a map
to no underworld,

barren fields,
quarry of disrepair

my broken gem.
ruby.

II

SHADOWS OF CRANES

Children folded the colored paper
until it flew everywhere:
cubby rooms, corridors, front office.

1,000 cranes in the auditorium flitted
on quiet breezes of exhalation. Cranes
for a girl who couldn't get to class.

Through the hospital's plastic tent
she saw birds thick and lustrous
like her mother's voice.

They dipped, swirled, trilled.
On her last breath
they soared.

Students took on other projects,
Halloween bats, robins for spring.
Yet shadows of cranes remained:

some saw them float to class.
Assemblies heard faint cries,
the flutter of wings, a migration.

Baking It Out

connective tissue in flour, egg,
fundamentals of earth and animal.
i see them in my hands.

my friend's cancer in nodes,
firmament of body
so vast it can't be found

blender on high spatters chocolate.
i could make it stop,
wipe away every errant mark.

i could not lie down, put one arm
behind my head, press fingers
against breast

i blend batter lumps, scoop smooth mounds
onto buttered trays. richness
brings me to my knees.

GROWTH FROM GARDEN BOOKS AND EMAILS

Don't forget to water. —*Sunset Magazine*
Remember to pray. —D. D.

for B. D.

The gardener
should always plan ahead.
We have difficult news
to share with you.

Critical things are sunlight,
proper amendment to soil.
We're told that treatment
for this cancer is intense.

After you find the right spot,
you must care for your plant.
We will do everything we can
for our son.

Deep watering when young
enables trees to bear fruit.
Not everyone told us
about sterility from treatment.

Prepare to protect them
with hot caps in late frost.
He called the chemo
dragons of fire.

Surround a patio with pastel
for tranquil outdoor living.
The room was always dark yet
he felt the presence of his friends.

Breath of Heaven (Coleonema)
is a good option.
He said he was so tired,
even breathing was work.

Severing the branch
may not yield result.
Surgery at this point
was too dangerous.

Before you plant,
trim off damaged roots.
He couldn't understand why
they didn't cut everything out.

Even earth
may diminish.
*We tried
every alternative.*

Eventually they wither and die,
but only after months of show.
*He felt so weak
but he was strong.*

Don't forget
to water.

PLASTIC SWORD

for C.E.S.

Our booth barely blocks the din of chatter
(wedding shower? baby?) that surrounds us.

Maura leans in. I stare at velvet whisps of hair
that just grew back, remember strands floating

like filaments from blossoms on a breeze.
She says she'll go short this time before chemo.

Last night her youngest found his plastic sword,
vowed to slay cancer. The oldest had homework.

Joe's away on business but voice-mailed
We'll win.

I'll be there, I offer,
hands in my lap heavy

from the weight
of talk.

Looking Through
a Book with Friends

in memory of Lynn Kohlman

bare
with no breasts
bald head in sepia slopes

one gasps

chick has more guts
than i ever did,
jan tells the bandana story

when her scarf slipped in class,
a voice behind her exclaimed
heads have bumps?

dana's curl cascade
claire's thick bun
my blond blanket

so much to lose

light around the subject
is unfiltered.
i almost can't look

Chemo Wait

by the dark scream tv with
glowing growths

my friend waits

(white space
paper sticks to skin

bathrooms have lines
and stink

cold dreams flow from fluoride
planets at each chair)

for nothing more than outside,
careless breath of late afternoon,

bland sidewalk, scent of stray mustard
from an empty lot

(old woman near her has a slow drip,
no companion. never weeps—

studies me with crinkled eyes.
squeezing her blanket and doll)

Why No One Does Hospital
Reviews Like Movie Reviews

best parts:

when they used the blanket warmer

when hall floors were so shiny you could
glide but never slip

when the woman's cheek sported curls of onion
from a friend's bagel

worst parts:

when they wouldn't reveal the secret

when moans from other rooms
caressed the covered guerney

at the end how the woman said
planes took off all night long
but hers was grounded

Travels

dying does not bother me
she professed
after loved ones she'd lost
returned in dreams
with photos of their new locale.

why the tears, then,
the catch in the throat.
flushed, wide-eyed,
as though caught in regret
as the train moves on.

CHILDHOOD FRIEND'S
OUTDOOR SERVICE

At parties I won the peanut hunt.
Other children stopped to suck salt,
guess at nut numbers.

Maybe just gaze.
Pastel clad, I skittered across lawns
in zig-zag patterns for hideout spots.

Not seeking prizes or envy—
just brown bags torn with abundance,
evidence of effort's success.

Today's gathering holds no hunt.
All in black, we laud one
who sought every medical miracle.

Hundreds who cheered her on
stand stunned.
At her plot I clutch my bag.

III

HUNGER AT THE OFFICE

why would one
who loves the body
binge and purge?
she tells me her needs
might translate to sex.
hunger abates with nightly
hook-up guys,
sometimes their dorm,
sometimes mine, kind of
like a midnight snack.
she leaves my office,
i am famished.

Doing My Job

> A shrink who has candy in bowls,
> delightful music playing, handknit
> afghans on the couch, and a tendency
> to complement you on everything from your outfits
> to your high I.Q. is not doing her job.
> —AMY BLOOM, O: *The Oprah Magazine*

She walks down the hall with a fistful of wrappers.
Sorry I ate so many, Doc, but you kept me waiting
and my mood is blue.
No worries! I say. *Chocolate can be therapy!*
Come on in!

The woman throws herself on my couch,
resumes the story where Mom forgot carpool.
Music of the moment is Gaelic, those dancers with a beat.
Her foot taps in time as she recalls Mom wouldn't apologize,
then baked cookies for weeks, as though compensation.

I remember my favorite recipe with bittersweet chunks.
She says *Could you could turn down the music?*
I simply nod and smile for clinical significance.
How smart of you to notice my music!
I declare, after the important pause.

No, really, she says. *It's getting on my nerves. I feel shaky.*
I suggest the afghan, *Why don't you pull it up all the way?*
When she does her shoes stick out. *Manolo Blahnik!* I observe.
She blushes, *Oh thank you, but they're fakes.*
Frauds. Just like me! She begins to cry.

Well, they look authentic to me, I reply,
suggesting she return to cookies, what kind they were,
all the important details. When she can't remember,
I encourage fantasy, free association about sugar, butter.
The music crescendos, I feel vibrations of the dancers' stamps.

But Doctor, I feel really overwhelmed, she says.
*The chocolate in my stomach, the music, the itchy blanket,
the randomness of cookies and my mother . . .*
Brilliant! I say. *You are so incisive! Exactly! See you on Thursday!*

Imagined

I.

room of soft pillows,
candy in bowls
not for comfort.
this space cradles
brutal sounds of self,
what must be heard,
what said. no ease.
calyx of primal bloom,
language almost forgotten.
laid bare in word.
in name. letters
plain as day.

II.

some begin
to hear
within.
to string
phrases
as colored
beads,
patterns
of new
design.
some
hold out
creations,
consider
their
imagined
worth.

Lost and Found

dream my office is veiled in tulle
of word, what was said

not past but here,
layers of lost and found

my mother got lost in gown and wrap,
sheaths of tears from steam

in the child's sick room, sitting
long after sleep

everything moist when i woke,
she rocked said mother, mother

as though i weren't there
as though the one she wanted were

climbing into folds saying mother
wanting to be that

layers she rocking
called mother

then her eyes on me
i believed i was there to her

mother in that moment
the place i found

LEGACY

therapist asks the mom to look at her daughter.
mom's body triangles away from her child,
space between them immense.

the girl twists in a bony repose
of skinny t's, thread bracelets around vivid
scars on wrists, eyes searching her mom's face.

blind mom. can't look at her child cutting
to feel less dead. mom's vision
is the dishonest daughter she herself was,

the one who covered up everything.
out of sight, out of mind
all these years.

Hindu Wish Bracelets

They say hope happens
if they loosen. Molly
wears hers in convolutions
of yarn, angst macramé.
Miniscule bells in string twists
cover the burnt red
of stitched wrists.
So many wishes
to unleash the hold
of Molly's work.

SYLVIE

Sylvie punched the girl who squirted
pomegranate on her new jeans.
Sylvie just earned them from babysitting.

Sylvie hit hard, ripped
the girl's stupid "I love Pugs" shirt.
Upset everyone at school.

Sylvie just discovered
cutting. *It's so cool
when the pain goes away.*

Sometimes Sylvie stays on the bus
until the final stop. Pretends
she's the last person on earth.

No demons or destruction, everything
just blank, barren. She has to make it
on her own. In this silence, she does.

Gardening on the Job

She sought help to tame the weeds within.
Therapy was soil prep: if you don't address your dirt,
nothing grows. She wore overalls, I wore my suit.
We excavated fallow fields in fifty minute blocks.

Hoeing, weeding, tilling *ad infinitum*.
Rhizomes where harvest should have been,
our toil a havoc of thought. Break-through
was my prize orchid, the day I revealed its deceit.

I showed her how silk petals on hidden wires
covered real buds that someday would emerge.
How things are not always what they seem.
Light and water on my couch, laughter

in magnificent green. She announced
I need no longer stand in for her.
I itched and withered in my creamy white;
she walked out the door in full bloom.

BE YOU

in bed again
with the buddha master,

stumble-reading *peace is every step*
while his feet touch mine.

come on, honey!
no. you're too cold.

come on I need you.
listen to me!

wind shushing against panes
like when earth moves

i listened all day,
my ear aches.

i cover myself with pages
and chant; he won't desist,

his feet grow warm,
everything warm.

my feet are numb,
invisible,

i can't find them,
can't find any of me.

my book has fallen somewhere—
i try a command.

your turn, help me get back!
oh honey he says,

drifting off in buddha-talk,
just be you.

IDEA OF MEAN

to Marin Sorescu

Some say our sole possession
is ideas. True wealth:
the idea of sky.
Such free thought

opens up the world.
I could make earth
a house of worship,
stars my midnight snack.

Who says people are mean!
Let us alter the idea.
People have clumsy wings,
webbed feet that tangle and trip

when trying to advance.
In feeble beings,
ideas of mean
dissipate.

We're awkward ducks,
backward birds
with inflated brains.
Top-heavy with the possible.

IV

FEASTING

The child's tree people walked to work, school,
morning tennis lessons in stylish burrs, silky leaves.

Birch bodies, birch lives. Everyone looking happy
despite. Shouting. Hitting.

Some touching where they shouldn't whispering *I'll kill
if you tell.* Twig-Town.

A few sticks felt
they couldn't go on.

Felt no one in the whole grassy world understood.
Thought about jumping off a high branch, overdosing on sap.

One twig stayed in all day and cooked. At evening,
the scent of her stew and bread drove everyone wild with longing.

Nuts and pods stopped their business call or yoga class
to return home, hoping her earthly delights might be theirs.

Most had meager stone suppers. Yet in dark dirt
everyone dreamed of feasting.

Mornings she found them asleep, hard to rouse,
not wanting to face the day.

HOMAGE TO A PERFECT HYMEN

Graduating girls
must wear white,
tea-length,
no spaghetti straps.

Seven here know the other side of sex,
three gave it up to a bike. Four starved
until they didn't bleed
but everything fit.

Flowers! Each graduate's sweet bouquet.
Sitting, cross your legs, rest it in your lap,
decorum is your responsibility,
don't put other girls to shame.

Aren't they pretty whisper parents. Satin, tulle,
ringlets, ribbons. Tied up tight in white.
The commencement speaker in Royal Blue
floats veils of words, *the sky your limit.*

A breeze ruffles hair and lace,
rain spots dark on dresses like stains.
Parents gasp, some girls smile.
Soon a torrent takes over,

chairs tip, some shove
as everyone bolts for cover
except the girls, crossed legs,
cradles of bloom.

BALLET GHOST

once she painted her dance
from memory of the studio mirror,

its silver screen a movie for one.
wielded oils in dense delicious smudges—

thumb and brush-frosted thighs
like cakes of rich peach-meat.

unabashed flesh in childhood acrylic
faded, flaked.

she no longer dances
or paints

avoids reflections
of the bone feast

skin stretched taught
against its frame,

canvas without creator,
dancer without dance.

Sex at the Mall

First he told her to do it behind a mini-cruiser
in the lot. It made her want one,
so compact, almost invisible.
You could weave in traffic, escape.

Next time near Claire's Accessories
behind the artificial tree. She half-watched girls
in the piercing chair, decided she liked pink earrings
with dangly hearts, how they swing.

After school he wedged her in the corner by Sees,
rows of chocolates like babies in ruffles.
Women in white handed out samples,
each a surprise. *Don't use your hands*, he said.

Liberation to find she couldn't imagine taste,
velvet slide on the tongue, delight of dark scent.
She watched kids unwrap little pieces from a shiny bag,
discovered she didn't feel a thing.

Student Found Dead in Dorm Room

Leaves outside her window
with the edges of fall, a cool wind

like back home in Ohio, this is not home,
this is all she ever imagined.

Schedules, curricula, plans
she can't fathom anymore,

biochemical imbalance or not.
She lays down after pills,

watches oaks and maples.
First day of class.

My son in the next dorm is stunned:
I saw her around. How could she?

On the same day his sister
goes to her first junior high lunch,

tries to sit with three different cliques.
Each group gets up. Her pink backpack

comes home heavy, baggies of sandwich,
cookie, apple still sealed.

She says she wants to rest on her bed.
She looks out the window at trees.

Outside the Fort

She watches them build, for hours
they collect stones scattered across the beach.

Large, round. Walk among them like giants,
striding, stepping through, deliberating.

In his arms each holds phenomenal weight.
In her arms an infant wrapped in pink.

The boy's shorts are blue, the man's lime-green.
They sling at a circle drawn in sand.

Each heft a heavy thump. They stack piles, large to small.
Symmetry of their construction against disarray of beach

stands like night against day. Tower of stones.
When finished they squat in the center, smiling,

blue and green. Outside she places sandwiches, fruit,
cups on a small table, carries pink.

HOMELESS WOMAN

All day the commuters hold their nose
before they pass, her sheen of dirt,

matted hair, dancing hands a sign.
She does not sit on the bench to babble.

She masters myths, strange tales
where birds sculpt air, children

sing in their sleep. Legends of fire,
flood, houses built from bone flow through her,

rivers of different current, same source.
Circle back to the start.

Destination is the end of each story,
which welcomes the next. Hers.

Suburban Legend

She starved for years.
No bread, packets
of low-cal dressing in her purse.

Sculpted by lifting weights,
welcomed knives on her face.
Hurt for beauty.

She doesn't tell about home,
her knees, devotion to babies.
The story is ghost, a woman she was.

Young, plump, unkempt. Sitting in a kitchen
filled with dishes to wash, clothes to fold.
She cradles a thick pen. The notebook fat.

Hand, shy of the open page, scripts a narrow tale,
legend of danger. Loving the words so much,
she doesn't see the story she writes.

HOCKNEY'S CELIA

The clavicle with shade,
one stroke, quick, black
for depth on a bare frame.

She reclines, looks down
not in shame but meditation,
mouth sorry for nothing.

Dishes jostle in the kitchen.
Child ghosts, a man at her temple,
calling, commanding.

Thread of flat dark paint
winds around longing.
I succumb to curve of arm,

heft of thigh, abundance of a woman
who fills the space of her life
with her own lines.

LANGUAGE OF BIPOLAR

One single cycle spans her life.
Starts dark, curtains drawn against light
that spins too fast. So much to cry about:
food, weight, babies, men, wine

with no song. Black conundrums.
Crawls through years until planets
reverse course, re-align their arc.
New language begets worlds with words

as fire and air. Some call her speech
blather, how she pronounces *you* instead of *ego*,
I in place of *id*. Sings ballads about satisfaction,
the yes of breathing, of lying down then rising up.

The shrines are insane. Stacked with fetishes—
baby shoes, trainer bras, misplaced keys.
Wears them around town on foot,
declares herself "fleet." High speed thoughts

zoom to glory places, play riff games
with terms (*Ore of essence. Essential orgy*)
until everything expands. Paints mantras.
Love begins at home. Amo, Amas, Amat

in wondrous oil. Chants on bended knee
to all art, all she has nourished and renamed.
What others call *crazy*
she calls *free*.

Masterpiece

For decades suppressed libido manifested obsessions
with art shows, their fashion and wine.
Everyone in drag, drunk off pretense.
Climaxing spanky spaces with canvas and string.

Dreams became vivid oils that caressed and stroked,
rendered self in florid forms of fantastic adoration.
Mornings, love bruises bled branches of bronze,
violet nimbus of the gods from sternum to pubis.

Her final year she unveiled herself to opening crowds,
skin rippling, shimmering like metal under a torch,
sculpted to a new sheen, new configuration
of joint and plane. Malleable with every desire.

V

Second-Hand

i devour accounts of moms
who ironed sheets or smashed berries
into jam: housekeeping as art

i crave antique tea-cups
with narrow gold lips, quilts stitched
from dresses in checkered blue

give my girl her meds then bid on-line
for vintage aprons, earthen bowls, wooden spoons
follow second-hand recipes with big eggs

bulge with quilts, cups, casseroles
cook and browse and cook
like there's no tomorrow

CHAMOMILE

against the cadence of sleep
afternoon
broad with light

less pain

i watch tree skeletons,
winter
without end

through the orchard
a yellow tray with steamy cups,
pastel mints

touch
my daughter's hands
mine

chamomile
for sleep
so tired of sleep

look beyond
bed
the body

her face
a mirror
my eyes sky

hers earth

Dr Yuan

I.

exiled after he cured gorbachev's wife

i heal your girl

hands across body shadows

not chi. cosmos. chi
a plane. this rocket

i began to believe
in redemption

II.

after one hour

everything faded
you had to pay again to ride

some came three times a day.
i ran out of faith before money

having to remember, again and again,
what she'd lost

Baskets of Potatoes

wore mourning gowns, tripped over raw
fruit, peaches, plums i could not eat.
hunger stole taste of bread.
of wine. outside birds, violets
consumed merciful dark

sat in cellars with baskets of potatoes
stubbled with age, scraped their peel
against dank dirt until babies appeared
in moonlight, dazed. slept, ate skin,
drank barley with mint. silence swaddled.

first crone came quietly, pulled edges of sun
off windows, wove cocoons, insisted we crochet,
twist rosemary, birdnest into ropes of light
we flung against the past. found they held.
climbed.

try the riding cure,
let my girl mount a big horse,

gallop off into chaparral and big sky.
what is chaparral, how do people

· take charge. drive forever to stables
where they yell *come on in,*

unlatch gate, leave me out.
she walks among animals

the size of dreams.
fences and space,

no waiting room.
i slip off shoes,

feel corral dirt,
splintered sun-hot rail.

birdsong, smell of barn, imagine
being her right now, feeling

power of legs against beast.
she is out of vision, everywhere

light fragments, breaks apart the world,
i can't tell what fits

i hold on

SANCTUARY ON LAKE STREET

Vivid darkness in a stout white mug
slides a bit on linoleum,
yellow with black specks, still moist.
Mesmerizing hand waltz of the waitress

swiping at intervals.
Steam, bitter shock to the tongue,
solid sticky touch of cup.
Body heat a hug.

Below a smoky TV the cook
flips burgers, grins at replays.
I pretend the woman two stools down
is my mom.

She studies her pie and fork
with such tenderness,
as though meringue
came from God.

Pilgrim

hands sun-spattered,
veins blue criss-cross.

knees sort through silt
for weedroot and rock,

dirt nestled under nails.
back hurts a little,

arched over beds of blossom.
no matter to hands,

their own in dark grit,
sifting to satisfaction.

hard to explain to those
who do not worship.

Earthbound

to Joy

On my skin hot her hands.
Dark bird soars away.
Bones exult. Empty house
of blood and heart.

She says my body
yearns for this void.
She says carry stones.
Kneel to earth. Gather:

magnolia, maple, plum.
Weave a crown, a cord
for your robe of light,
your robe of petal and root.

Hers green fields, pants clay,
blouse pond. Seeds, buds,
scent of early bloom
fill my vessel.

Bound to earth,
to all it sends forth,
all it takes away.

Vipassana

ten breaths a small field to sow.

i thought i learned to scatter seed

long before these exhalations.

sit, breathe, count. release soil

around seeds, start over when lost.

lifetime of breathing

in every breath, ontology

of seed. sing labored

birth one to ten,

blooming awake.

Trumpet Ghosts

Small hands cupped bulbs,
swollen seed as miracle
in a child's eye,
every narcissus possible,

every spent bloom a new start.
We bent over earth,
scraped dirt with fingers, brushed
tender underside of arm against grit

to smooth beds of bulbs.
She wiped smudges from her fever
with leaves, never knelt in dirt again.
The year of no bloom, I see her.

Thin green reeds without bud sway
in fragility, trumpet ghosts
that shadow the garden wall.
I watch her gather every one.

New Meds

before, she says,

i went through door
after door
to find a thought

now thoughts
share the room with me

sitting in sun
as anyone
on a spring day

AT *Crafts Galore*

We find one purple wig,
$2.99 Special. Sally coils
the harvest of her brown,
tucks it under shock of grape.
Her face blooms
to plush peony.

I need to try. It accommodates
the complexity of my ruminating head
and quirky blond. I become a sassy
sweet pea, a ruby moon hyacinth.
For once I offer the world
tendrils and vines.

Who knew I could grow in an aisle
of fluorescent lights and slippery floors.
Mom, what's up with you,
I remember when we read
Jack and the Bean Stalk, believed
transformations happen anywhere.

VI

After Sun

what follows, what precedes:
scattering of sun on banks of oaks

flying from swings at lacy park
taste of green sky, laughter, blood

seeing our son for the first time
outside of me, his wordless song

twenty years later
the mottled farewell of skin

even now, so late you must leave,
the memory of you

exceeds this rush
of mouth against hand

Last Day

Sounds of summer rain above us,
smell of wild fennel from the field.

Before bed he promised pancakes,
blueberry with syrup from the farm.

I'm convinced that soon he'll sit up,
grasp his dad's old robe, walk barefoot.

I see the kitchen, the bowl with berries.
His hands. Some visions almost a memory

that precedes, as though one can be sure
of certain things. His tall frame in the robe.
Early light.

NEST

woven   empty
   with   of
      everyday   abyss
         books   for
          sweaters   but
            nightlight   last
              morning   to
                light built

Memory of Beslan School

Chechen militants take over School Number One
in Beslan, Russia, where more than 1,100 students,
teachers and parents become hostages. Three days
later, two explosions rock the school and Russian
forces launch a chaotic rescue. In total, 333 hostages die.
                    —*CBC News in Depth: School Shootings*

Hostages ate dahlias,
nibble of petal,
bitter with earth, redolent of bread

TVs bloomed children
with first day bouquets,
hostages ate dahlias

Mother's violet heath shrouded
vine of dead son, broken bud
bitter with earth, redolent of bread

I touched my tongue to late summer
zinnias, sky hue at dawn
hostages ate dahlias

convinced that plants could sustain,
gardens, meadows, any place
bitter with earth, redolent of bread

Elders keened over fields of death,
fragrance of rose, blood,
hostages ate dahlias,
bitter with earth, redolent of bread

Myth of Horizon

Years between us: scattered starling formations.
As though farewell rain is news: no need to announce.

Hawk in the kitchen. At breakfast, death in the sink.
She couldn't fly home.

Love travels well? Baggage gets misplaced
on the open road.

Starling's bough of wet blooms I cut from the Judas Tree—
across our bed, tears.

Photos of the dead float like birds on my screen.
Birds of sunset. Flames across what horizon.

Forecast is red flag.
Fountain offers dreams (At night I thirst for sleep).

Morning, no desire. Sparrow flits, sings wet.
Hawks circled above. Some said spirits came for you.

The butterfly bush shelters remnants of gold wings
from non-warriors.

I look to the sky for signs.
Clouds, birds won't reveal.

Gravel at my feet. The meditation garden
makes a lot of noise.

Outside darkness. Traffic echoes or ocean?
Tulip's reckless blooms defy winter rain.

Again, nightly news.
Yet somewhere I hear song.

Just the Night

they hear each other breathe,
the dog outside

barks at a possum,
then howls, then

the possum's low hiss.
he gets up, brings the dog in,

she listens to his reprimand
in the dark. silence,

neither sleeps,
as though a voice might call out,

a bad dream or fever
or simple fear.

there are no voices
except for the dog

ASTRAL

nights i fly with branches of trees,
taste color of sap

each breath of bitter wood a world

tangled blooms, bony arms
mirror your embrace

i am caught

by my bed i pack bags,
perfumes, scarves, hoping

to run into you

GOLD

outside our window,
hive-removal men cut
into richness so immense
it's a threat

beauty of bees madness
to those who have no room
to share: we need our house
to hold

shutters close,
their angled wood
yields slats of light
across your back

complicated comb mutes
drilling, hard penetrates
soft. words give way
to peculiar tones,

delicious as night
against day. wrap around
the sweet. not evening
or dawn. lyric of gold.

THIRST

what slakes the thirst of drought?
each day, rain from head to toe

desire remains: *i long, i long*
the train's cry,

its muffled voice echoes
what no storm satisfies

trees' wet roots search the sky,
surprised by their weight

world heavy
from thirst

FINAL HORTICULTURE

last vision:
faces of the kids

their dad as well,
holding our dogs if space is tight

background: beach i love
my garden, of course, in front.

while i wish to see it at its best,
dry patches and weeds would suffice

the unfinished
my open invitation.

Awake at the Holidays

Darkness, steady thrum
of a storm we longed for,
hymn to slake thirst.

I want to dream about simple things,
ingredients for almond bread,
lavender bands of plants.

Holidays we used to make:
parties to end a week. Or begin it.
So much to celebrate.

Tonight with grown children home,
husband not on the road, I decide
to stay up, string lights, bake.

SPOKES

Woman dancing
in the wheel of life
finds her skirt caught
in spokes.
She is held.
Upside down,
sideways,
then upright.
Bruised, bleeding even.
Yet the world
from new angles
makes sense.

TULIP TREE

Late afternoon blooms
flew around me.
Then sun went east—
my evening sky
shocked with light.

At night Mom called
from that place
beyond birds and trees.
What's it like over there?
I begged. *Are you happy?*

The sky, the bird, the way
you learned
to breathe.
Her reply so loud
I had to laugh.

LATITUDE

love in the grass-wet below
trees, desperate end-of-day love

green shade. trees
in the veins of your hands we arch

like branches that find
the forgotten sky

our fingers and teeth
carve names onto blonde bark

jajera. eucalyptus, not our names
as though we could forget trees

as though we no longer need *you*, or *i*,
only desire to name the world

BIOGRAPHIC NOTE

Lisa C. Krueger's previous collection of poetry, *Rebloom*, was published by Red Hen Press in 2005. She also has written a series of interactive journals related to psychology and creativity. Her poetry has appeared in numerous publications. As a clinical psychologist she maintains a private therapy practice focused on women's issues, writing therapy and the role of creativity in wellness. She lives in Pasadena with her husband and three children.